D1522282

What
Jesus
Does

31 devotions about Jesus
and the Church

SINCLAIR B. FERGUSON

TRUTHFORLIFE®
CF4•K

10 9 8 7 6 5 4 3 2
Copyright © 2021 Sinclair B. Ferguson
Hardback ISBN: 978-1-5271-0731-1
Ebook ISBN: 978-1-5271-0855-4

Reprinted in 2022
by Christian Focus Publications,
Geanies House, Fearn, Tain, Ross-shire,
IV20 1TW, Scotland, U.K.
www.christianfocus.com
with
Truth For Life
P.O. Box 398000
Cleveland, Ohio 44139
truthforlife.org

Cover design and page layout by
James Amour
Printed and bound by Gutenberg, Malta

Scripture taken from the New King James Version. Copyright © 1982 by Thomas Nelson, Inc. Used by permission. All rights reserved.

CONTENTS

INTRODUCTION

If you go to church or Sunday School, you have maybe heard grown-ups speaking about how important it is to spend time each day with the Lord Jesus, and to think about him.

I don't know about you, but I find it hard just to sit down and think. Sometimes my head feels empty. But then, at other times, it feels as though there are too many things to think about! So, it's not easy just to sit down and say to yourself, 'I am going to think about Jesus for the next five minutes.'

What helps me is when I have something to think about—something that makes me think! So, reading a book helps me. Or if someone asks a question. It's a bit like starting the engine in the car—something needs to turn the key or press the starter button. You read and then you start thinking. Or you hear the question and you try to work out the answer—so you start thinking! I have tried to put these two things together in this book. I hope that reading it will start you thinking about Jesus. In addition, since each of its chapters begins with a question, I hope that will help you think even more about him. Don't forget to ask for his help by using the prayers.

When I was at school we hardly ever spoke in class. We spent a lot of time writing. So I find writing helps me to think. Not everybody likes writing. But if you do, why don't you keep a little book and write down your thoughts about Jesus while you are reading this book? Who knows, maybe one day you'll write a book like this one!

But until you write your own book, I hope you will enjoy the one I have written for you!

Sinclair B. Ferguson

1. DOES JESUS KNOW YOUR NAME?

Lord Jesus,
help me to think about you, learn
more about you, and love you today.

READ: JOHN 10:1-11

Who are the only people you know you don't call by their names? Have you worked it out? Yes, it is your mum and dad! If we have aunts and uncles, we call them by name, don't we? But mum is just mum or mom, isn't she? And dad is just dad.

The Lord Jesus tells us that we can call him by his name. But he also tells us it works the other way round. He calls us by our name too!

Jesus tells us that we can think about him as the Good Shepherd. The shepherds Jesus knew gave their sheep names. Don't you think that must have been fun? And it was a good idea too. If you have a dog, or a cat, it has a name, doesn't it? If you were with a group of people whose dogs were all barking loudly, it wouldn't help if you shouted to your dog, 'Dog! Quiet!' He wouldn't know which dog you were talking to! So, it's a good idea to give your dog a name. Shepherds looked after a lot of sheep—so giving each one of them a name was a good idea. What do you think would be some good sheep names?

If Jesus is the Good Shepherd, who do you think his sheep are? Yes, all of us who trust and love him. And listen to this: Jesus says, 'the shepherd ... calls his own sheep by name' (John 10:2-3). He knows exactly who you are! He knows everything about you. And he loves you.

But here's something interesting you might not have thought about. In the very last book of the Bible, Revelation, chapter two, verse 17, Jesus says this about everyone who trusts him: 'I will give him a white stone, and on the stone a new name written which no one knows except him who receives it.' Jesus has his own special name for each of us! Nobody else knows it. It means we are special friends. And when we see him, he's going to say to us, 'Promise not to tell anybody. Here is my new name for you. It's written on this white stone.' Amazing! Maybe someone will ask, 'What name did Jesus give you?' But it'll be a secret between him and you!

Lord Jesus,

How much you must love us to think up a special name for each of us. Help us to listen to your voice each day. Thank you for your amazing love.

Amen.

2. WHAT KIND OF WATER DOESN'T COME IN A BOTTLE?

Lord Jesus,
help me to think about you, learn
more about you, and love you today.

READ: PSALM 63:1-8

Did you know that if you don't drink water, you get thirsty and then get sick? A big word for this is 'dehydrated'. But it's not just your body that can get dehydrated. Your soul can get dehydrated and sick too.

One day Jesus had been walking for hours. He was thirsty. He sat down beside a well around midday. But in Jesus' day you needed to lower down a bucket to get water out of a well. And of course, Jesus didn't carry a water bucket around with him! However, when he looked up, he saw a woman carrying a great big water bottle.

Now, you wouldn't go out to a well all on your own at the hottest part of the day, would you? Jesus thought, 'There must be something not right with this woman's life. I think she has a dehydrated soul. I will ask her for a drink of water. But she needs the kind of water only I can give her. I am going to talk to her about it.'

Jesus was right. He could tell that the woman coming to the well had a dehydrated soul. What do you think that would look like? She needed to drink the water of God's love.

When she arrived, Jesus said, 'Would you let me have a drink of water, please?' As they began to talk, she realized Jesus knew all about her dry and sick soul. He said to her, 'If you knew who you were talking to, you'd be asking me for the water of God's love. If you drink some of it, your soul will be healed.'

At the end of the conversation the woman went back to town and told everyone they needed to meet Jesus. Many of them believed in him!

Lots of people seem healthy. You see them walking around with a bottle of water in their hand. But inside their souls are all dried up. They are not drinking the water that only Jesus can give them. Nobody can put this water in a bottle and sell it in the supermarket. Only Jesus can give it to you. Let's ask him, 'Lord Jesus, will you give me a drink of your water, please?'

Lord Jesus,

We know we need to drink from the water of God's love. Please help us to do that so that we can taste it every day. We want to be healthy Christians.

Amen.

3. DO YOU HAVE AN OLDER BROTHER?

Lord Jesus,
help me to think about you, learn
more about you, and love you today.

READ: MARK 3:31-35

My mother kept a special box that belonged to her big brother who was called Donald. He was my uncle. He died a long time before I was born when my mum was just a tiny little girl. He fought and was killed in the First World War which happened between 1914 and 1918.

In the box was another box—a smaller one. There were some medals in it. When I was a little boy, I loved to open the box and look at those medals. I own this box now and sometimes I look inside it again. The medals in the smaller box are more than a hundred years old. When I look at the medals, I think about my mum and about her big brother who died. It reminds me of another brother who fought in a greater battle and died.

Can you think who that might be? Yes, we all have a Brother who fought in an even greater war for the whole wide world – the Lord Jesus.

The Bible tells us that when Adam and Eve sinned the whole world fell into the hands of our enemy, the devil. Jesus called him 'the prince of this world'. And the loving apostle John wrote that the whole world lies in his grip. We need someone to defeat him, because he is our enemy. But we are all his prisoners of war. We can't free ourselves! We need to be rescued.

The good news of the gospel is that the Lord Jesus came to fight back against the devil. During his life he kept on fighting him and winning. And then, when Jesus died on the cross, the devil must have thought he had managed to defeat him. But he was wrong!

Jesus knew that his Father had planned his death as the only way to defeat the devil. The plan was this: Jesus, God's Son, would die for our sins on the cross. As a result, he took away all our guilt, and all our shame. By doing that he destroyed the power the devil had over us since the time of the Garden of Eden! Jesus won a great victory. Then he rose from the dead. That's why we love him so much.

So, we have an Older Brother who died for us, the Lord Jesus Christ. He is always with us.

Lord Jesus,

Thank you that you came to fight the devil and defeat him for us. And thank you that you want to forgive all our sins as well. Help us to trust and love you always.

Amen.

4. DO YOU HAVE ANY BROTHERS AND SISTERS?

Lord Jesus,
help me to think about you, learn
more about you, and love you today.

READ: 1 JOHN 3:1-3

Here's a riddle to solve. I have four children. One of them has more brothers than any of the others. Which one of our children is it? Have you got it? Yes, it's my daughter! My wife and I have only one daughter. She has three brothers. Our sons have only two brothers each!

Now here is another question about brothers and sisters. Sometimes we get on better with one of our brothers or sisters than we do with the others. But could it ever be right in a family to love one brother more than the other brothers and sisters?

Don't you think the right answer must be 'No'?

But are you really sure? Would I have asked that question if it was as easy to answer as that? No. It was really a trick question. Everyone who trusts in the Lord belongs to another family as well—the church family! And in that family there is one Brother we all love more than anybody else, isn't there? The capital letter tells you who he is, doesn't it? Yes, Jesus.

The Bible teaches us we can think of the Lord Jesus as our Great Elder Brother. We all love him best of all because he has loved each of us more than anyone else ever can. And because we all love him best, and he has loved each of us so much, we want to love each other too! So, we don't love each other less because we love him more. We love each other more because we love him most of all!

When we think about this, it can help us to love people in our church family we find difficult to get on with. Don't forget that maybe they find you difficult to get on with too!

If we love our Great Elder Brother, Jesus, he will put love into our hearts for everyone he loves. So, if there's anyone in your church family that you find difficult, imagine Jesus introducing them to you. What would he say? 'This is James. I died for him. He's your brother.' If Jesus died for him, don't you think he wants to help you to love him too?

Lord Jesus,

Thank you for being our Great Elder Brother and for dying on the cross for us. Help us to remember that you love everyone in our church family.

Amen.

5. WHO LOVES CHURCH?

Lord Jesus,
help me to think about you, learn
more about you, and love you today.

READ: JOHN 17:20-26

Do you love church? Do you like the building? What do you think about the seats? Are they comfortable? Is there a carpet on the floor?

Do these things really matter? Of course they matter. But they are not the most important things, are they? In fact, did you know that the New Testament uses the word 'church' over one hundred times, but not once about a building? When it uses the word 'church' it always means the people who belong to the church.

So, the most important thing about loving the church is that we love the people. We enjoy being with them—the young people and the old people. Did you know that some of the old people are really, really interesting? Here's a good thing to do: say to an older person, 'Will you tell me your story, please?'

We love the church. But who loves the church most? Maybe it's the minister, if you have one. Perhaps you have elders and deacons. Could it be them? Well, they should love us all very much. But they don't love the church most, do they? So, what is the answer?

The answer to the question is: Jesus! How do we know Jesus loves the church most of all? Because he died for us all on the cross and then rose again to be with us forever.

When we love Jesus, and he is our Friend, then we want to tell him, 'Lord Jesus, what you love most of all is what I want to love most of all too.' And we ask him, 'Lord Jesus, help me to love my church because it's your church'.

Next time you are at church, take a look at the people. They're all different. Are some old and some young, some big and some small? Isn't it wonderful to love all these different people? And remember, when you go to church there will be people looking at you and thinking, 'We really love you because Jesus loves you so very much.' That's why we love church!

Lord Jesus,

We thank you that you love your church. We thank you that you died for us and that you are alive. Please help us to love you and all the people in our church.

Amen.

6. WHAT'S HE REALLY LIKE?

Lord Jesus,
help me to think about you, learn
more about you, and love you today.

READ: REVELATION 1:9-18

Have you ever asked about someone—maybe somebody famous—'What's he like?' I have met one or two famous people, and if other people find out they always ask: 'What's he really like?' or 'What's she really like?'

Have you read the book by C. S. Lewis or maybe seen the movie: *The Lion, the Witch and the Wardrobe*? It is about what happens in a land called Narnia. Some children enter it through the back of a wardrobe. In Narnia it is always winter but never Christmas, isn't it? If you have read the book, you'll probably remember the part where the children first hear about Aslan. One of them asks this question, 'What's he like?' and is told that Aslan is a lion! Lucy, one of the children then asks, 'Is he safe?' And Mr Beaver replies: 'Who said anything about safe? 'Course he isn't safe. But he's good. He's the King, I tell you.'[1] Jesus is like that.

In the last book in the Bible, Revelation 1:14-17, John, who wrote it, describes a vision he had of Jesus. He described him like this: 'His head and hair were white like wool, as white as snow, and His eyes like a flame of fire; His feet were like fine brass, as if refined in a furnace, and His voice as the sound of many waters; ... out of His mouth went a sharp two-edged sword, and His countenance was like the sun shining in its strength.' John tells us that he fell down before him as though he had just died!

Does that sound safe to you? It doesn't sound very safe to me! But then the Lord Jesus showed John just how good and kind he is. In fact, John tells us Jesus showed him he is as safe as safe can be. Because there is nowhere safer in all the world than being with King Jesus.

Later on, in the Book of Revelation, John saw Jesus again, but this time in a different way. Someone told him to look at Jesus and he would see a Lion. But when John looked, he saw Jesus standing there looking like a Lamb. Jesus was the Lamb of God who died for our sins. John knew he was safe. We are all safe with him!

---

1. C.S. Lewis, *The Lion, The Witch and the Wardrobe* (London: Collins, 1980, revised 2009), page 75.

Lord Jesus,

We know you are so strong and have so much power. But we know you are also good and kind. Thank you for wanting to keep us safe.

Amen.

7. WHICH IS MORE DIFFICULT?

Lord Jesus,
help me to think about you, learn
more about you, and love you today.

READ: MATTHEW 6:5-15

Do you think some things are more difficult than others, and some things are easier? What do you think is more difficult, being a girl or being a boy? Which is more difficult, to be a woman or to be a man? Which do you think is more difficult, to be a mum or to be a dad?

Since I'm a father, maybe I should stick to talking only about that!

What is a father? How does a father find out what he is supposed to be? Here's the answer the Bible gives. Who was the very first father? Yes, it was God himself! He is called 'Father'. God lets us use the same word to describe a dad as we use about him. Do you think that's maybe because he wants every father to live in a way that will remind his children of God the Father?

Do you know what that makes us dads want to say? You can probably guess. It makes us want to say, 'Oh help, that's not easy.'

It isn't easy, because we dads are far from perfect. But we know our Heavenly Father loves his children; so we dads want to love our children too. Our Heavenly Father provides for us; so we dads try to provide for our children too. Our Heavenly Father teaches us through his Word, the Bible; so we dads want to teach our children his word too.

But here's something important. Our Heavenly Father wants us all to become more and more like the Lord Jesus. He knows that is the best thing in all the world. And so he has to train us, and he has to get rid of everything in our lives that isn't like Jesus. Sometimes that hurts. But he tells us in the Bible that it is just like the pain sportsmen and women feel when they are in training. It may feel sore, but it makes us strong. God is training us to become like Jesus!

Dads who love their Heavenly Father also want to train their boys and girls to become more and more like the Lord Jesus. Maybe that will sometimes feel sore to us. But it's the only way we will grow strong. Honestly, that's true!

Heavenly Father,

Thank you for our homes and families, and for dads and mums who love us and want us to be like Jesus. Help them to be like you and help us to be like Jesus.

Amen.

8. WHAT DO YOU KNOW ABOUT JESUS' FAMILY?

Lord Jesus,
help me to think about you, learn
more about you, and love you today.

READ: MATTHEW 13:53-56

What is it like to live in your family? If I were to ask you, 'How many brothers and sisters do you have?' what would be the answer? 0? 1? 2? 3? 4? Even more than that?

Do you ever think about what it was like in Jesus' home when he was growing up? How many brothers and sisters do you think he had? Or do you think he was the only child in Joseph and Mary's family?

See if you can work out the answer from these verses: Matthew 13:55-56. Jesus had been preaching to huge crowds of people. He was famous. Then he went back to his hometown. Everybody was talking about him and wondering how this had happened. They knew his family! None of them was famous. So they asked this question: 'Is this not the carpenter's son? Is not His mother called Mary? And His brothers James, Joses, Simon, and Judas? And His sisters, are they not all with us? Where then did this Man get all these things?' Can you do the sums?

Brothers: James+Joses+Simon+Judas = 4
Sisters: 'All'. How many is all? 'sister'=1; both sisters=2; all his sisters=?
We usually say 'both' when there are two. But if we say 'all' we usually mean at least three!
So, here's the question: How many were in Jesus' family?

Answer: Joseph and Mary, plus four brothers, plus at least three sisters = nine people. So there were nine. Is that right? Have you forgotten Jesus himself? Ten people, maybe more! Do you think that would have been fun? You could almost have your own football team!

They all got to know each other really well. And here is something wonderful to think about. Jesus' mother, Mary, trusted him as her Saviour. And James his brother called him 'our Lord Jesus Christ'. Probably they all came to trust him. And they knew him best of all.

Lord Jesus,

We thank you that your family, who knew you best and longest, came to trust in you. Help us to trust in you, with everyone in our family too.

Amen.

9. DO YOU COLLECT AUTOGRAPHS?

Lord Jesus,
help me to think about you, learn
more about you, and love you today.

READ: ROMANS 5:1-5

Do you know what an 'autograph' is? It's a signature. Some people collect autographs and get people to write their names down on a piece of paper or in a book. Sometimes they sell them for a lot of money— do you think that's right?

When I was in school everyone in our class had an autograph book in which we tried to collect the autographs of famous people. The problem was we didn't know any famous people. So, we just signed each other's books!

Do you think anyone ever got Jesus' autograph? That would be the most valuable autograph in the world, wouldn't it? Imagine owning the autograph of the Lord Jesus!

I think you can still get Jesus' autograph, but he doesn't write it with a pen and ink on a piece of paper. He does it another way.

One of the most infamous queens of England was Queen Mary or Mary Tudor. She loved the country of France. Mary said that if somebody were to cut her open they'd discover that 'Calais' was written on her heart. That's a bit gruesome, isn't it? But Mary didn't mean that 'Calais' was written on her heart with a pen and ink. She meant that she loved it because she loved France more than anywhere or anything else.

Jesus has a way of writing his autograph on our hearts too. He does it through his Holy Spirit.

When the Holy Spirit works in our hearts it is like Jesus using a pen and ink to write. When he does that we can say something far more important than Mary Tudor said! We can say, 'If you could see into my heart, you would be able to read Jesus' name there. I love him more than anything and anywhere and anyone in the whole wide world!'

Is Jesus' autograph written in your heart? If not, ask him to write it there today.

Lord Jesus,

Thank you that you still write your autograph into the hearts of your children. Please write it in our hearts so that we will trust you and love you.

Amen.

10. WHAT'S A FAMILY TREE?

Lord Jesus,
help me to think about you, learn
more about you, and love you today.

READ: ROMANS 5:12-17

Do you have a family tree? In a church I belonged to there was a lady with a very grand sounding name who had the biggest family tree I have ever seen. I don't mean the kind of tree that grows in the garden of course. It was like a huge map with names on it, all joined up by lines. It told you which son or daughter belonged to which father and mother, and whose father was their grandfather and great-grandfather and great-great-grandfather. The lady with the very grand sounding name was at the bottom and the lines stretched right up to the top.

People like to trace their family tree because they want to know where they came from! But sometimes they discover what they call 'the black sheep of the family'—someone who did something terrible or spent the family fortune! To think that money might have been yours!

In Jesus' time family trees were so important to people that they even memorised them as far back as they could go. Because of that, we know Jesus' family tree! Here is something really interesting about family trees. Did you know that if you were able to trace your family tree all the way back, you would find someone in it who was also in Jesus' family tree? Can you guess who it might be? Let me give you a clue: he was 'a black sheep'.

Could it be King David? No, it's not David. What about Abraham then? No, it is someone even before Abraham! Perhaps Noah? Someone even before Noah! Who then was it?

Here is a clue: he was the very first 'black sheep'. Yes, it was Adam, the first man. We all belong to his family tree. We all inherit our sinful hearts from him. But the sinless Son of God, our Lord Jesus, entered this family tree from the outside. He didn't inherit any of Adam's sinful nature! And because of that he was able to obey God—the very thing Adam failed to do. And then he died on the cross for all of our sins. And now he's started a new family tree—the Jesus Family Tree. And if you trust him, your name is in it!

Heavenly Father,

This is an amazing story about these two family trees. We want to belong to the new family tree of the Lord Jesus. Please write our names in it.

Amen.

11. WHO ARE YOU LIKE?

Lord Jesus,
help me to think about you, learn
more about you, and love you today.

READ: ROMANS 8:28-30

One day we were sent a photograph of one of our grandsons. When we saw it, my wife said to me, 'Look at that! He is doing exactly what you do.'

What do you think he was doing? When I'm a bit shy and don't know what to do, I still do something I did when I was a boy. I put my finger on the dimple on my chin and begin to play with it! Maybe my mum told me not to put my hands in my pockets! So here in the photograph was my grandson doing exactly the same thing I do.

Do you know what we call that? It's a family likeness. We pass them on. It might be the way we look, or something we do. People can tell what family we belong to.

When we belong to the Lord Jesus, we have two families, don't we? Do we have two sets of 'family likeness'? Yes, we do. People can sometimes tell what family we come from just by looking at us, or watching what we do, or by listening to the way we speak. Maybe they say to you 'You're just like your father' or 'You're so like your brother'!

Wouldn't it be wonderful if people could say that but mean we were like our Heavenly Father and like our Elder Brother the Lord Jesus? That would mean there was something about the way we talked to people, or about what we did, that made them think about God and his love.

The Bible tells us that our Heavenly Father wants to make us more like our Elder Brother the Lord Jesus. That could mean big changes, don't you think? Because we're not really like Jesus, are we?

However, here's something worth remembering. Usually other people are the first to notice the 'family likeness' in your life—you don't see it. It's the same when the Holy Spirit works in our lives to make us more like Jesus. You might be the last to notice! Yet, other people will notice. That's worth remembering. So, let's ask our Father to make us more like his Son!

Heavenly Father,

Thank you for taking us into your family. Now we pray you would make us more like your Son, the Lord Jesus, so that our friends will come to trust him too.

Amen.

12. ARE YOU FOLLOWING?

Lord Jesus,
help me to think about you, learn
more about you, and love you today.

READ: LUKE 9:21-27

Do you ever notice that sometimes people can seem to change and be different? Maybe they seem happier, or perhaps sadder than before. Isn't it interesting how you notice these things?

One day when Jesus' disciples were with him, they noticed that something about him seemed different. Recently he had started telling them that he was going to be rejected by the religious leaders and killed, and then resurrected soon after.

The disciples heard him, but they didn't really take in what he was saying. It didn't make any sense to them. Do you think they just didn't want to hear Jesus speak like this? I think so.

Soon afterwards they started heading for Jerusalem. They didn't think there was anything unusual about that. Jesus went there every year. But they thought they saw a new look in Jesus' eyes and on his face. Maybe he sometimes looked as though he was all on his own, just thinking—even although they were with him.

The time had come for Jesus to be rejected, badly treated, and crucified—and then rise again. He already knew that was going to happen. I can't imagine what it must have been like for the Lord Jesus to wake up every day knowing that in a short time he was going to suffer on the cross. It must have been on his mind a lot. And it must have been hard for him.

Maybe that's why he told his disciples that following him would not be easy for them either. It would mean they would also share in his sufferings. The disciples didn't really understand what he meant until after the resurrection.

Jesus also said this would be true for anybody who became his disciple. You will find his words in Luke 9:23: 'If anyone desires to come after Me, let him deny himself, and take up his cross daily, and follow Me.' If we live near to Jesus, we will experience opposition for his sake. I wonder, then, are you willing to follow him?

Lord Jesus,

You have suffered so much because you loved us. We pray that you will help us to be willing to suffer for you because we love you in return. Please help us today.

Amen.

13. HOW CAN SISTERS BE SO DIFFERENT?

Lord Jesus,
help me to think about you, learn
more about you, and love you today.

READ: LUKE 10:38-42

Do you know any families where there are two sisters? Have you ever noticed how different from each other sisters can be?

When Jesus went to Jerusalem he sometimes stayed in a little village nearby called Bethany. He really enjoyed visiting a home there where his friend Lazarus lived with his two sisters, Mary and Martha.

Lazarus, Martha, and Mary were all different from each other. The Lord Jesus cared for each of them. That meant sometimes he would talk to all of them together, and sometimes he'd have something special to say to each of them.

One day when Jesus was visiting, Mary was sitting listening to him. Martha was in the kitchen trying to prepare all kinds of food for a special meal. I don't know what happened—maybe she spilt something or burnt something?—but I think we would say she 'lost it'! She stormed off to Jesus and began to complain about having to do everything herself. 'Don't you care?' she said to him. 'Don't you care that Mary's sitting here listening to you while I'm slaving away on my own in the kitchen?'

Imagine saying, 'Don't you care?' to Jesus! Martha wasn't the first to do that, was she? Remember how the disciples woke Jesus up when their boat was caught in a storm on the Sea of Galilee? They said the same thing. They forgot that the reason Jesus came into the world was because he cared so much! But Jesus calmed both storms! He helped Martha see that he wanted her to be with him and listen to him—even if it meant just having a sandwich for dinner!

On other days Jesus showed his special care for Lazarus and for Mary. But what Jesus said to Martha has a lesson for us, doesn't it? Some days we get so busy doing things that we forget to sit down and spend time with Jesus, when that's what we need most of all!

Lord Jesus,

Thank you that you love each of us. And thank you that you speak to each of us through your word, the Bible. Help me to spend time with you and to listen to you.

Amen.

14. WHAT IS A DISCIPLE?

Lord Jesus,
help me to think about you, learn
more about you, and love you today.

READ: LUKE 14:28-33

Do you know what the word 'disciple' means? It comes from the Latin word 'discipulus' which means someone who learns from another person. We are Jesus' disciples!

Being a disciple is like going to a school where the Lord Jesus is your very best teacher! We go to school to learn things, don't we? But in your school you have books to help you. The book Jesus used to teach his disciples was the Old Testament. He didn't own one—that would have been far too expensive. So, he memorized lots of it. He maybe even learned it all by heart! Isn't that amazing? So, when we are Jesus' disciples, we learn from Jesus' book.

At school you get tests. Do you know why? Is it because your teachers are horrible and don't like you? I hope not! No. They want to make sure you have really learned. Sometimes, Jesus gives us tests too. He wants to see if we've learned what he has been teaching us.

A man once asked Jesus to teach him how he could know who his neighbours were so that he could obey God by loving them. I think he was hoping Jesus would tell him his neighbours were only people he liked! Instead, Jesus told a story about a Samaritan who helped a Jewish man who had been robbed and injured. (The Jews didn't like the Samaritans!). Then Jesus said to the man who asked the question: 'Now you go and follow the example of the Samaritan!' What a lesson!

I once spoke about that story in church. Later that evening, when I was going somewhere, I saw a large bundle lying on the ground. What do you think it was? I went over, and discovered it was an old man, a tramp! He needed help. Just that afternoon I had said to my friends, 'Now that we have heard Jesus' story, he will probably test one of us to see if we were listening'. Do you think maybe Jesus was testing me? I think he was saying, 'Were you listening to what you said earlier today?'

Jesus' disciples learn to do two things: to listen and to do. Do you want to be a disciple?

Lord Jesus,

Thank you that you are not only our Teacher, but you are our Friend. Help us to listen to what you teach us in your word, and then help us to obey because we love you.

Amen.

15. CAN BAPTISM MAKE ME CLEAN?

*Lord Jesus,
help me to think about you, learn
more about you, and love you today.*

READ: ACTS 8:26–39

Do you think the water that's used when there's a baptism in church can make us clean inside?

I once bought a bottle of shampoo that said it was so good it would put clean thoughts in my head! Do you think I believed that? Are they still making that shampoo? You can't put clean thoughts in your head by washing your hair with shampoo, can you? Shampoo can't wash away our sinful thoughts. Sinful thoughts are a different kind of dirt, aren't they?

When we baptise someone, we use the same kind of ordinary water we use with the shampoo. It usually comes out of the tap! Can that water wash our sinful hearts clean? No, of course it can't. Our sinful hearts have a different kind of dirt in it than water can wash away. They need to be washed with something much stronger than water!

Does being baptised matter then if it can't wash our hearts clean? Is it important? Yes, it is. After all, Jesus told us to do it, and everything he says is important! What does baptism mean, then? It is a sign we can see of something we can't see.

Think about it this way. When a young man wants to marry the young woman he loves he may give her a beautiful ring to wear on her left hand. It's called an engagement ring. He will spend as much as he can afford to buy it! But there's something about it even more important than its beauty or how much it cost. The ring means something. It's a sign the young woman wears that tells you she is engaged to be married to someone who loves her more than anything else in the world. It says, 'I love you with all my heart and I want you to have my name'.

Baptism is like that. It's a sign that Jesus loves us more than anything else in all the world. It's a sign that he wants to wash our hearts clean from our sin. And it's a sign too that he wants us to have his name! We are baptised into the name of the Father and of the Son and of the Holy Spirit. The water can't cleanse your heart. But the Lord Jesus can. And he will if you ask him.

Lord Jesus,

There are many different signs in the world that say many different things. Thank you so much for the special sign of baptism that tells us you love us more than anything.

Amen

16. WHY DID GOD MAKE MOTHERS?

Lord Jesus,
help me to think about you, learn more
about you, and love you today.

READ: JOHN 14:18-24

Have you ever wondered how God thought up the idea that you would have a mother?

Can you imagine what it must have been like when there was absolutely nothing except God? God was absolutely everything and God was all there was. There was nothing else—and nothing wasn't anything! It's hard to imagine, isn't it?

So God thought up everything when there was nothing to start with! What an amazing mind God must have. He thought up elephants and giraffes and mountains and stars! But why would God think it was a good idea to make mothers? Was it, perhaps, so that there would be children?

Is that the only reason? When you were very little, did you wash your own clothes? Did you make your own meals when you were a baby? Think of all the things your mother has done for you. Each of them is a reason why God thought it was important to think up mothers and then create them. That is why we are so grateful for them.

But here is another reason that you've maybe not thought about before. Watching a mum or a mom helps you to understand what the Holy Spirit does! God is so much greater than we can imagine. There is only One of him. And yet he is God the Father and God the Son and God the Holy Spirit—three Persons and yet only one God!

We know about what the Father and Jesus his Son have done. But what does the Holy Spirit do? In John 14:23 Jesus says he comes to make our hearts a home for him to live in along with his Father. Of course, if the Holy Spirit does that he must be there too!

My mum was always tidying up the mess I made and making sure that we all felt at home. She comforted me when I was hurt and cleaned me when I was dirty. That's what mothers do.

A mother is also called a 'homemaker'. The Holy Spirit is a Homemaker too. He does in our hearts what our mother does in our house. He cleans and tidies us up for God to feel at home with us!

Lord Jesus,

Thank you for the way our mothers help us to feel at home! And thank you that the Holy Spirit works in our hearts so that you and the Father will feel at home there too.

Amen.

17. DO YOU EVER PESTER GOD?

Lord Jesus,
help me to think about you, learn
more about you, and love you today.

READ: LUKE 18:1-8

Have you ever noticed that when it gets warm little insects start flying around? Some of them can be really annoying, can't they? Especially if they bite. Fancy wanting to eat you! Then we feel they have become a nuisance. We call them 'pests' because they pester us. Some people are like that too, aren't they? They're pests and they pester us!

Do you ever pester people? Maybe you pester your parents. You say, 'Can I have this?' But they say 'no'. And then a couple of minutes later, you try to get it another way. Do they give in?

There is a story in Luke 18:1-8 about a widow woman. Someone had done something wrong to her. She didn't have her husband to help her. So, she asked a judge for help.

Now this judge wasn't a nice man. He didn't love God, and he didn't like the people who asked for his help. But the widow kept coming to him and asking him for help. She just wouldn't give up. She kept pestering him! Eventually he thought, 'She's going to keep on doing this. I don't care tuppence for her, but I'd better help her or she'll never stop'. So he helped her.

Does it seem a bit strange that Jesus told a story with an unjust judge in it and a woman who was a bit of a pest? What was the point he was making?

Jesus sometimes told 'It's Like This' stories. They explained how God's kingdom works. And sometimes he told 'Much More' stories. A 'Much More' story is where Jesus says, 'If this is what happened in the story you can be sure that God will do much more than that!' This was a 'Much More' story. Do you see his point? In the story the unjust judge gives a widow what she asked for because she kept asking for the right thing. In real life, if you ask God for the right things, for what he wants you to have—you can be even more sure he'll answer you!

Heavenly Father,

Help us to ask for what you have promised to give us, and help us please to keep on asking. Thank you that you know what we need even before we ask!

Amen.

18. WHERE DID YOU COME FROM?

Lord Jesus,
help me to think about you, learn more
about you, and love you today.

READ: PHILIPPIANS 3:3-11

Do you know where what you are inside came from? A lot of what you are on the inside comes from your family, doesn't it? But that can be complicated! After all, each of us comes from two people and two different families. Then before those two families there were other families. If you keep going back it can get very complicated!

As far as I know, most of what is inside me has come from Scotland! But I only ever saw pictures of my two grandpas, and I knew only one of my grandmas. So, I was never able to ask, 'Where did you come from?' I have always thought that most of what's inside me from the past is all from Scotland. But you never know, do you? Unless you get a DNA test. DNA tests are amazing because they can tell you all the different bits and pieces that make you who you are!

The apostle Paul didn't need a DNA test to tell him where he was from. His family had kept very careful records all the way back to a man called Benjamin and beyond. Do you know who he was? He was the son of Jacob and his great-grandfather was Abraham!

Do you ever have to learn lists of things by heart? When Paul was a little boy he would have had to memorize a long list of his family's names going all the way back to Abraham. And then he had to learn more! He learned the names from Abraham back to Noah's son, Shem. And then from Shem right back to ... who do you think? Yes, Adam!

Paul knew where he came from right back to Adam. Think of all these people in his family who had known God's promise that he would send a Saviour. Many of them had trusted God and had believed that one day the Saviour would come. He did. His name was Jesus of course.

Many people in Paul's family tree had believed God's promise about Jesus. But, at first, he tried to harm those who believed in him. His family tree didn't make him a believer. That's a big lesson for us, isn't it? We need to come to trust in Jesus for ourselves. Do you?

Lord Jesus,

It is a big help to us to know that so many people believe in you. But help us to trust you for ourselves. Thank you for the love you have for me.

Amen.

19. ARE YOU ASKING THE RIGHT QUESTIONS?

*Lord Jesus,
help me to think about you, learn
more about you, and love you today.*

READ: PSALM 119:9-16

Have you noticed how often people ask questions? It's one of the ways we find things out, isn't it? When you meet someone for the first time one of the ways you get to know them is by asking them questions: Who are you? Where are you from? What do you do?

It's important, though, to ask the right question, isn't it? Because if you ask the wrong question you will probably get the wrong answer! Here is a silly example. If you ask somebody 'What does green smell like?' they might say, 'Stupid! I can't answer that question. Green doesn't smell; it is a colour!' But if you ask, 'What does that green flower smell like?' They might say, 'It smells very nice' or 'It smells like freshly mown grass.' Then you would have asked the right question and received the right answer.

It's the same when you are reading the Bible. Have you ever thought of asking the Bible questions when you are reading it? It really helps to do that.

When I started reading the Bible for myself, I learned some good questions to ask. They helped me understand it better. They also helped me to see how to serve the Lord better.

Here are some of the questions:

1. Does this passage in the Bible tell me something about God, and who he is, and about what he has done in the past, and about what he is doing today?
2. Does this passage tell me something about the Lord Jesus and how much he loves me?
3. Does this passage tell me anything about my sin and how God has promised to forgive me and change me?
4. Does this passage tell me what to do in order to live for Jesus?

So, questions are good. Why not ask some of these questions next time you are reading the Bible? I hope they will help you as much as they have helped me!

Lord God,

Thank you that there is so much to learn from your word, the Bible. And thank you that when we ask it questions it answers us! So please speak to us through your Word.

Amen.

20. WHO IS THE GREATEST?

Lord Jesus,
help me to think about you, learn more
about you, and love you today.

READ: JOHN 13:1-14

Did you know that Jesus' disciples sometimes argued about which of them was the greatest?

I wonder if you like looking at paintings. One of the most famous painters in the world was a Dutchman called Vincent van Gogh. He painted around nine hundred oil paintings during his short life. He must have painted at the rate of a painting every week!

When Vincent was alive, I think there was only one person who ever wanted to buy any of his paintings. She paid him four hundred French francs. But today people spend millions and millions of pounds to buy his paintings. Imagine if your great-great grandfather had bought all nine hundred of Vincent van Gogh's paintings and then you sold them today.

You wouldn't be able to live long enough to count your money!

So, people today believe that Vincent was one of the greatest artists who ever painted. But in his own day nobody believed that. The people who looked at his paintings just couldn't understand what he was doing.

Have you ever been sure you were right and then discovered you were really wrong? Sometimes what doesn't seem very great to people turns out to be the greatest. And often the things that people think are the greatest turn out not to be. People can get it wrong.

Does that remind you of anything? It reminds me of the Lord Jesus.

The prophet Isaiah wrote in chapter fifty-three of his book, that when the Saviour came, people wouldn't recognise him. They would look down their noses at him and reject him. That happened, didn't it? The Lord Jesus was rejected and crucified. Yet all the time he was The Greatest! And God showed that by raising him from the dead. He crowned him as King!

However, here's something else for us to learn: Jesus, who is The Greatest, said the way to be great is to serve others. If that's true, would anyone say about you, 'He's great' or 'She's great'?

Lord Jesus,

You are The Greatest! Thank you for loving us and dying on the cross for us. And thank you, Father, for proclaiming Jesus to be King. Help us to serve like him.

Amen.

21. HOW DID SIMON BECOME PETER?

Lord Jesus,
help me to think about you, learn
more about you, and love you today.

READ: JOHN 1:40-42

Do you remember the very first time you met your best friend? The disciple called Simon never forgot the first time he met the Lord Jesus.

I think Simon saw himself as a leader. Every time we read a list of the disciples in the Gospels he is always the first one to be mentioned. And he was usually the first person to speak up. Even when we read about Jesus' three special friends, Simon's name always comes before the names of James and John. Some people are just like that, aren't they?—first in everything.

One day Andrew, Simon's brother, brought him to meet Jesus. What would Jesus say?

Jesus said, 'So you are Simon the son of John?' Isn't it interesting that he didn't say, 'So you're Simon, Andrew's brother?' I wonder if he knew about him without Simon knowing it! But then he said, 'You shall be called Cephas.' Where Jesus lived people usually spoke a language called Aramaic which was like Hebrew. The word 'cephas' means a stone or a rock. Petros or 'Peter' is the same word in Greek.

What did Jesus mean? Why would he say 'You are Simon... You shall be called Cephas'? I think he was telling Simon that now that he had met Jesus everything was going to change! And we know that it did. But it wasn't easy, was it?

'The Rock'—big, strong, reliable—that was quite a nickname to give Simon, wasn't it? But he turned out not to be very strong. He was sometimes weak, and he often said the wrong thing. We know that he denied Jesus several times. He was 'The Rock' that sometimes crumbled. But when Jesus first spoke to him, he wasn't telling Simon what he already was, but what he would become in the future. Jesus was saying, 'I know who you are; but I also know what I'm going to make you.' That was a long process. But at the end Simon became a rock!

The Lord Jesus wants to change you as well. Let him do that today.

Lord Jesus,

Thank you that you see us as we are, and still love us. Thank you that you also see what you are going to make us and do with us. Please do all you want in our lives!

Amen.

22. DO YOU 'READY, STEADY, THINK'?

Lord Jesus,
help me to think about you, learn more
about you, and love you today.

READ: ROMANS 12:1-8

Do you have races at school? Perhaps your school has a sports day. In our school we had an 'Egg and Spoon Race'. You had to hold an egg on a spoon and run. The winner was the person who got to the finishing line first with the egg still on the spoon. And then there was the 'Three-Legged Race' when you tied your left leg to someone else's right leg and tried to run as though you were one person with three legs!

I remember all of the races began in the same way. The starter would say, 'Ready, Steady, Go.' When we were older the serious races began with the starter saying, 'On your marks; Get set' and then he would fire a pistol in the air!

In one of his letters, Simon Peter says being a Christian is like taking part in a race. He wants to help us to run well. But he starts us in a different way. He doesn't say, 'Ready, Steady, Go.' He says, 'Ready, Steady, Think!' That's a bit different, isn't it? Don't just 'Go', but 'Think'. What does he mean? Why do we need to think? Because if we don't think, we may end up not doing well in the race!

Here is something to think about when we are making decisions. It makes no difference if the decisions are big ones or small ones, here is a question that will help us 'Ready, Steady, Think'.

Will my decision about what to do bring pleasure to the Lord Jesus? If the answer is 'I don't think so' that really helps us not to do it, doesn't it? But how do we know what brings pleasure to him? We find the answer in his word, the Bible. So, that means we will want to know our Bibles better! That's why Psalm 119:105 says: 'Your word is a lamp to my feet and a light to my path.'

So, let's make sure we get to know our Bibles better. That will help us to 'Ready, Steady, Think'. And then we will give the Lord Jesus pleasure. He loves it when we do that.

Lord Jesus,

Thank you that you have given us your Word to guide us. And thank you that it tells us what gives you pleasure. We want to give as much joy to you as we can!

Amen.

23. ARE YOU AN HEIR?

Lord Jesus,
help me to think about you, learn
more about you, and love you today.

READ: 1 PETER 1:3-9

Do you remember being born? Did you help to create yourself? No, you didn't. You brought nothing with you into the world —not even baby clothes! But when most of us were born we became part of a family. Here is something you didn't know then. Perhaps you don't even know it now. When you belong to a family you become what is called an 'heir'. That means that when the older people in your family die, what they own will be shared out among the family members. What is left to you is called 'an inheritance'.

Now if you think only about the amount of money and things you might get, that sounds good, doesn't it? But there are some things you need to know.

One of them is that the government might take some of the money in taxes!

And did you know that money can lose its value? Most people today get paid about twenty-five times what they got paid when I started working. But a lot of the things you buy cost twenty-five times as much! When I was small you could buy twenty big chocolate bars for one pound. Now you would have to pay more than one pound to buy one of them!

Things also wear out, don't they? Some things get rusty and stop working. Things get broken and can't be repaired. So an inheritance can get spoiled, and its value can fade away.

There is another kind of inheritance, however. Peter talks about it in 1 Peter 1:3-5. He says that we have been born again as Christians into a family with a different kind of inheritance. It can't perish, or go rusty, or fade away. It is being kept in the Bank of Heaven so that it will never lose its value. And, he says—in case you're worrying: God is keeping it for you, and he has promised to keep you so that you eventually enjoy it!

What could this inheritance be? It's Jesus. 'You've not seen him,' Peter says, 'but you love him, and one day you will see him.' What a great day that will be—if you are an heir! Are you?

Lord Jesus,

You are more valuable to us than the whole wide world! Thank you for bringing us into your family and giving us an inheritance that will last for ever.

Amen.

24. DO YOU EVER HIDE?

Lord Jesus,
help me to think about you, learn more
about you, and love you today.

READ: PSALM 130:1-8

Why do we hide? It might be because we are playing the game of Hide and Seek. But sometimes it is because we have done wrong. We don't want anyone to find out. We cover ourselves up by hiding. Or sometimes we try to cover up and hide the wrong thing we have done.

When our children were very young we often had a bowl of fruit on the table. We said to them, 'If you want to eat an apple you need to ask for permission first.'

One morning I went into the dining room and picked up an apple from the bowl on the table. I got a big surprise! But what surprised me was quite small! Somebody had taken a single bite out of the apple.

I then picked up another apple and turned it round. Somebody had taken a bite out of that apple too. So, I picked up another apple, and then another, and another…. Every single apple had one bite out of it! Somebody in the house had eaten the equivalent of an apple without eating a whole apple! And then he had turned all the apples round in the bowl so that nobody would notice He had crept out of the room and gone upstairs into his bedroom!

Why did he not just leave the apples in the bowl in a way that we could all see the bite marks? And why did he not own up? And did he really think we would never find out? Was he telling himself inside 'I didn't really eat "an apple"; I only took a small bite out of each apple. So, I didn't really disobey'? He knew we would discover the truth. But he still hid the apple bites.

I smile when I remember that day. I smile because I loved my son even when he was naughty. But I smile too because I think we're all like that with our Heavenly Father, aren't we? We try to hide from him the sinful things we do. And we try to hide ourselves too. But deep down we know better, don't we? We know we can't hide.

What we forget is that our Heavenly Father loves us even although we sin. Have you forgotten? Then this would be a good time to say 'sorry' to the Lord and to ask him to forgive you and to change you.

Heavenly Father,

You see us every moment of every day. There is nowhere we can go to hide from you. We are amazed you still love us, and that Jesus died for us. Thank you for your love.

Amen.

25. WHAT IS JOY?

*Lord Jesus,
help me to think about you, learn
more about you, and love you today.*

READ: JOHN 15:1-11

What do you enjoy doing? Do you enjoy eating ice cream? Do you enjoy reading? Do you enjoy playing games? We all enjoy something, don't we?

Why do some boys enjoy cricket but not football or rugby? Why do some girls enjoy netball but not hockey? Why do you enjoy being with your friends, but you know that others in your school don't like them very much? Sometimes it's difficult to explain why you enjoy being with someone, isn't it? But enjoying someone means that when you are with them, you feel that there are good things happening.

Have you ever noticed that when you are enjoying something, or enjoying being with someone, you usually aren't thinking about yourself all the time? Something bigger has happened to you.

Jesus said that he gave us all his wonderful teaching so that we would enjoy being with him. I think that means he must also want to enjoy being with us! Can you imagine him saying, 'I think I would enjoy it if you and I spent time together'? That's amazing.

Here's another interesting thing. Have you ever noticed that when you enjoy being with someone the time seems to pass quickly? But if you are doing something you don't enjoy time seems to go very slowly. When you are on a long journey and it's boring you say to your dad, 'Dad are we not there yet?' But if you were on the same journey with your best friends and enjoying talking with them you would hardly notice the time. That's the way the Lord Jesus wants us to enjoy him, and he wants to enjoy us.

Is there a secret to having joy? When we were young we were taught that the right way to spell joy is: Jesus-Others-Yourself: putting Jesus first, then others, and only then yourself.

Here are some wonderful words of Jesus from John 15:11: 'These things I have spoken to you, that My joy may remain in you, and that your joy may be full.'

Lord Jesus,

You are a joyful Saviour and Friend. Thank you that you want to give us joy when we read about you in the Bible. Thank you for being with us every day.

Amen.

26. DO YOU HAVE ELDER BROTHERS?

Lord Jesus,
help me to think about you, learn more
about you, and love you today.

READ: 1 PETER 5:1-5

Have you ever noticed that when the Bible talks about the church it mentions some people called 'elders'? Sometimes it calls the same people 'bishops'. We don't have elders or bishops at school, do we? So, who are they, and what do they do in the church?

Perhaps if we think about what they are called, it will help us to answer that question. What do we mean when we say someone is an 'elder' brother or sister? We mean they're older than we are, don't we? They usually know a lot more than we do. They have had more experience of life than we have.

We look up to our elder brothers and sisters. We love them, we learn from them, and we want to be like them.

That's what an elder in the church is. It's someone who will be a really good big brother to us; someone we can look up to and think 'I would like to be like him.'

An elder is also like a big brother because he looks out for you and helps you. That's why the New Testament has another word for elders. It calls an elder a 'bishop'. The word it uses is the Greek word *episkopos*. If you look carefully at it, you will notice in the middle there are letters that appear in our words telescope and microscope. An *episkopos* is someone who looks out for you. If you say *episkopos* over and over again really quickly it begins to sound like 'bishop'!

So, what have we learned? The elders in our church are our big brothers who look out for us so that we will get to know the Lord Jesus better and know how to live for him.

The New Testament uses other words to describe what elders do. It talks about them as shepherds. We are like sheep sometimes, aren't we? We wander away from the Lord Jesus. So, he gives us shepherds to bring us back home because he wants us to be with him.

Did you know that in the Bible Jesus is called our Elder Brother, our Bishop, and our Shepherd?

Lord Jesus,

Thank you that you care for us so much that you have given us older brothers to look after us. We pray that you would bless them and our whole church through them.

Amen.

27. WHEN IS A PEN MORE THAN A PEN?

*Lord Jesus,
help me to think about you, learn
more about you, and love you today.*

READ: JOHN 1:1-13

Do you ever write with a pen? I have an unusual pen that was sent to me as a free gift! It's a pen, but it's more than a pen. It is also a little torchlight. So it's a pen, and a torch, and it's also a gift. It reminds me of what it means to be a Christian. How is that?

Well, what do we use a pen for? We use it to write. I use my pen to write letters to people. That's why this pen reminds me of being a Christian. Here is what Paul wrote in 2 Corinthians 3:3: 'You are an epistle of Christ'! Most people we know will never read the message about Jesus in the Bible. But Paul is teaching us that Jesus makes our lives like a letter to them saying, 'You need to find out about Jesus. You need to trust him as your Saviour. See what a difference he has made to my life.'

My pen is also a little torch that gives light. So, it shines in the darkness. That reminds me of Jesus' words in Matthew's Gospel chapter five, verse fourteen. He said to his disciples, 'You are the light of the world.' That means that when our friends look at us, perhaps they will think, 'I did not know I needed Jesus. But you have shown me I have been living in the dark.'

What was the third thing I said about my pen? Yes, it was a free gift! That reminds me of what Paul wrote in Ephesians 2:8-9: 'For by grace you have been saved through faith, and that not of yourselves; it is the gift of God, not of works, lest anyone should boast.' Our salvation is a free gift! Look at what Paul says about it:

Salvation comes by grace—we didn't do anything to deserve it. It is not our own doing—we don't get it by our own hard work. It is God's gift—so it is free! We can't boast about it because we didn't do anything to earn it. Jesus gives us salvation as a free gift!

So, my pen reminds me of three things: I am a letter from Jesus; I am a torch to give light to people; and my salvation is a gift from God.

Lord Jesus,

We thank you that you have made us a letter and a light to our friends to show them your love and to tell them your salvation is a free gift. Please help them to see.

Amen.

28. CAN YOU COUNT YOUR HAIRS?

Lord Jesus,
help me to think about you, learn more
about you, and love you today.

READ: MATTHEW 10:29-32

Do you like getting your hair cut? I don't! I once had my hair cut on a Saturday. On the Sunday lots of people said to me, 'You've had a haircut!' They said they liked it. But they were probably thinking, 'It's about time. You would think he didn't like getting his hair cut!'

But did you know that Jesus spoke about our hair? He did it twice. He said that if we think about our hair, we can learn some important lessons!

Here are some words of Jesus you can find in Matthew 5:36: 'You cannot make one hair white or black.' Is that really true? Some ladies change the colour of their hair! Yes, and some men too!

But after a while, the real colour of their hair comes back again! Sometimes they don't see it—it's quite hard to see parts of your head even with a mirror, isn't it? But everybody else can see that they must have dyed their hair! You can't really change the colour of your hair.

What did Jesus mean? I think he meant this. It's God who made your hair and its colour.

Then, Matthew 10:30 tells us something else Jesus said about our hair: 'But the very hairs of your head are all numbered.' Can you imagine trying to count your hair? Maybe there's a machine that can do it; but you can't, can you? Just look in the mirror. Try to count them. It's impossible.

What did Jesus mean? He had been telling his disciples that because they followed him they would experience difficult things. Some people would try to hurt them because they belonged to him. But they should not be frightened. They should remember that God was always watching over them. He sees everything. He cares not only about the big things but about the little things—and the little people too! He even knows how many hairs are on your head!

Your hair teaches you a lot! Remember that next time you look in the mirror or get a haircut!

Heavenly Father,

Thank you that you have made us and that you know everything about us, even the number of hairs on our heads. Thank you that you care so much for us.

Amen.

29. COULD THE CREATOR BE CREATED?

*Lord Jesus,
help me to think about you, learn
more about you, and love you today.*

READ: JOHN 1:14-18

Have you ever seen a new-born baby that has been really, really small—much smaller than usual? One of our sons is the kind of doctor who does operations on children and even on babies. I asked him one day, 'What's the smallest child you've ever done an operation on?' Do you know what he did? He held out his hand. A baby that small! Did you know that doctors today can do operations on babies even when they are still inside their mummy?

That's amazing. But here is something that I think is even more amazing. I wonder if you agree.

Do you know how big the world is? It's huge, isn't it? The Bible tells us that the world came into existence through the Lord Jesus. So, think about how great he is. He has amazing power. The Bible tells us God is so powerful he created the world as though all he used was his fingers. Imagine that!

So, what can be more amazing than that? Think about this: one day the Lord Jesus, the creator of the whole universe, came into the world he had made and was so small you could have held him in your arms—like Mary must have done.

Think of it—the One who put the stars in their places, and made the mountains and the oceans, the elephants, and the tortoises, came into the world he himself had made. He was just like you when you were a baby. He needed Mary to feed him, and carry him, and look after him. He needed Joseph to teach him how to cut wood and to make things.

If you have read the famous books about Narnia by C. S. Lewis you will maybe remember something Lucy says in *The Last Battle:* 'In our world too, a stable once had something inside it that was bigger than our whole world.'[1] That was Jesus! But why did he come to our world?

He came because he loved us. He came to show us what God is like in a way we could understand. And he came to die for our sins. What a wonderful Saviour he is!

---

1. C. S. Lewis, *The Last Battle* (London: Collins, 1980, revised edition, 2009), p.132.

Lord Jesus,

We can never thank you enough for becoming small and helpless when you were born and then being willing to die for our sins on the cross. We love you so much.

Amen

30. DOES GOD HAVE A FAMILY ALBUM?

Lord Jesus,
help me to think about you, learn more
about you, and love you today.

READ: REVELATION 21:22-27

I have a special photograph album that my big brother made when he was about nine and I was six. In those days we didn't have cameras on our phones! We had a camera called a Kodak Brownie 126. It took small black and white photographs. You put a spool of film into the camera, and took your photographs. Then you had to send the spool away and the photographs came back two weeks later. We don't have the camera now, but I still have the album of photographs.

Did you know that our Heavenly Father has a kind of family album that he keeps? I don't know exactly what it is like, but the Bible gives us some clues. The album is called 'The Lamb's Book of Life'. It is mentioned several times in the book of Revelation, the last book in the Bible. Here are three things we know about it:

It is a big book! Just the names of everyone in the Bible who trusted the Lord would be a lot, wouldn't it? If you added the names of everyone who has trusted the Lord since then it's no wonder the book of Revelation tells us the total is 'a great multitude which no one could number' (Revelation 7:9).

We know something else about this book: God wrote down the names of everyone in the book before they were even born. He knew that we would sin and that he would need to plan well in advance to save us!

The third thing we know about this book is its title. It is called The Lamb's Book of Life. Why do you think that is? Who is the Lamb? Yes, you know, don't you? It's the Lord Jesus. Do you remember how John the Baptist called him 'The Lamb of God who takes away the sin of the world' (John 1:29)? That's because he came to make a sacrifice for our sins when he died on the cross.

It's great to think that Jesus loves us so much that he gave up his life for us. And as a result, he has saved more people than anyone can count!

Lord Jesus,

We thank you that you want us to be in your family album along with so many others who have trusted in you and love you. Thank you for loving us so much!

Amen.

31. IS IT DANGEROUS TO BE A CHRISTIAN?

Lord Jesus,
help me to think about you, learn
more about you, and love you today.

READ: MATTHEW 5:10-12

Did you know that the governments of most countries make some laws to stop you from taking things that are bad for your health? The United Kingdom made a law that from 2016 all packets of cigarettes sold would have a warning on them saying, 'Smoking clogs your arteries.' They also said that the only colour that was allowed on the packet was the colour known as Pantone 448C! It's a shade of yellow that people voted the colour they liked least of all! It's a way of saying that smoking cigarettes is bad for people's health.

Those government health warnings make me think of a question. I wonder what you think about it. It's this: Could it be bad for your health to be a Christian?

It certainly can be dangerous! Sometimes, when the apostle Paul told people about Jesus, there were riots! Several times he was beaten with rods, and he was whipped. Once people tried to stone him to death! Another time he was shipwrecked and spent a whole night in the sea. Do you think it was dangerous for Paul to be a Christian? I think so!

In some parts of the world today, it is really dangerous to be a Christian. People will try to hurt and harm you. And even where we live it can be a bit dangerous. So remember Jesus has taught us that if we are going to follow him we will need to be brave. Because sometimes people may say things about us, or do things to us, that hurt either inside or outside.

But if that happens to you, it will be like being one of the first Christians, won't it? You can read the whole story in the New Testament book called The Acts of the Apostles.

But here are two lessons that will help us if we are ever in danger or are frightened, or if people say or do things that hurt us either inside or outside.

First, Jesus has given you a special promise: he will never leave you.

Second, when people hurt you, tell Jesus about it. He will help you. He's promised!

Lord Jesus,

We need your help to be strong, and to have courage. Help us always to be faithful to you. Help us to remember that you have promised to be with us always.

Amen.

Conclusion

Well, you have made it right to the end of the book! Well done! I hope you have enjoyed it and that it has helped you to think about the Lord Jesus, to trust him, and to love him more.

Most of the books I have written are for grown-ups. So why does someone who writes for grown-ups want to write books for children as well? There are lots of reasons, but since we're at the end of the book now, maybe I should mention only two.

The first is that when the Lord Jesus was on earth he loved children, and children loved him. And that's still true! He wants you to know that, and he wants you to trust him as your Saviour and love him as your Lord. Books about him can help us to do that. I hope this one has helped you.

The second reason is this. Although I am a grown-up, I was once one of the children who needed to learn about Jesus' love for me. And so, when I was your age, I started reading the Bible each day, and asking the Lord to help me to understand it. I hope you will do the same. The Bible is a big book—actually there are 66 books in it—and I needed help to read it and understand it. Two books you might find helpful are *66 Books One Story* and *Read With Me*.[1]

1. Paul Reynolds, *66 Books One Story*, (Christian Focus Publications, Tain, Ross-shire, Scotland, 2013) ISBN: 978-1-84550-819-7.
Jean Stapleton, *Read With Me*, (Christian Focus Publications, Tain, Ross-shire, Scotland, 2006) ISBN: 978-1-84550-148-8.

So I hope you will start reading the Bible when you are young. But try not to make the mistake I did! I thought that reading the Bible each day was the same thing as being a Christian. It was a while before I realised that although that's important, it's not the same as knowing and trusting the Lord Jesus himself. Then, one day, I was reading the words of Jesus in John's Gospel chapter 5 verses 39-40. He said to some people who were listening to him: 'You search the Scriptures, for in them you think you have eternal life; and these are they which testify of Me. But you are not willing to come to Me that you may have life.' I realised that Jesus was not just speaking to people long ago who made that mistake. I had made it too. He was speaking to me!

I knew then that I must pray that he would help me to come to him, to trust him, and to get to know him. Some time later, Jesus' words in John's Gospel chapter 8, verse 12 helped me to do that: 'Then Jesus spoke to them again, saying, "I am the light of the world. He who follows Me shall not walk in darkness, but have the light of life."' He has kept his promise!

So now you know why I wanted to write this book! And now I hope you will want to read the very best book—the Bible—yourself. Maybe you could start by reading John's Gospel.

May you know the love and presence of the Lord Jesus every day!

Sinclair B. Ferguson

Sinclair Ferguson has written this devotional book to help our children to think about Jesus and love him more. Its brilliance lies in the fact that it is so simple yet so creative. I can think of three great uses for it: (1) a gift for children to read on their own; (2) a guide for parents leading family devotions; and (3) a garden of homegrown illustrations for pastors to "pick and pinch" for their own children's addresses! Highly recommended!

Jonny Gibson,
Associate Professor of Old Testament,
Westminster Theological Seminary;
Author of *The Moon Is Always Round*

Have you ever felt disappointed? We've all felt the sadness of promises broken and dreams shattered. But here's the good news: Jesus keeps His promises, and He doesn't disappoint. He is with us every day. In this book by my friend Dr. Ferguson, you will learn to hope in the God who never disappoints or breaks His promises. This book reminds us that He is a God worthy of our love, and His people will go on loving Him forever.

Chris Larson
President & CEO
Ligonier Ministries

TRUTH FOR LIFE®

THE BIBLE-TEACHING MINISTRY OF **ALISTAIR BEGG**

The mission of Truth For Life is to teach the Bible with clarity and relevance so that unbelievers will be converted, believers will be established, and local churches will be strengthened.

Daily Program

Each day, Truth For Life distributes the Bible teaching of Alistair Begg across the U.S. and in several locations outside of the U.S. through 2,000 radio outlets. To find a radio station near you, visit **truthforlife.org/stationfinder**.

Free Teaching

The daily program, and Truth For Life's entire teaching library of over 3,000 Bible-teaching messages, can be accessed for free online at **truthforlife.org** and through Truth For Life's mobile app, which can be download for free from your app store.

At-Cost Resources

Books and audio studies from Alistair Begg are available for purchase at cost, with no markup. Visit **truthforlife.org/store**.

Where to Begin?

If you're new to Truth For Life and would like to know where to begin listening and learning, find starting point suggestions at **truthforlife.org/firststep**. For a full list of ways to connect with Truth For Life, visit **truthforlife.org/subscribe**.

Contact Truth For Life

P.O. Box 398000 Cleveland, Ohio 44139
phone 1 (888) 588-7884   **email** letters@truthforlife.org
truthforlife.org

CHRISTIAN FOCUS PUBLICATIONS

Christian Focus Christian Heritage CF4K Mentor

Christian Focus Publications publishes books for adults and children under its four main imprints: Christian Focus, CF4K, Mentor and Christian Heritage. Our books reflect our conviction that God's Word is reliable and Jesus is the way to know him, and live for ever with him.

Our children's publication list covers pre-school to early teens. We also publish personal and family devotional titles, biographies and inspirational stories that children will love.

From pre-school board books to teenage apologetics, we have it covered!

Christian Focus Publications Ltd,
Geanies House, Fearn, Ross-shire,
IV20 1TW, Scotland,
United Kingdom.
www.christianfocus.com

CF4·K
Because you're never
too young to know Jesus